# FLAT BROKE TO BILLIONAIRE

14 Best Ways & Top Tools To Make Money Online with AI in 2024 and Beyond

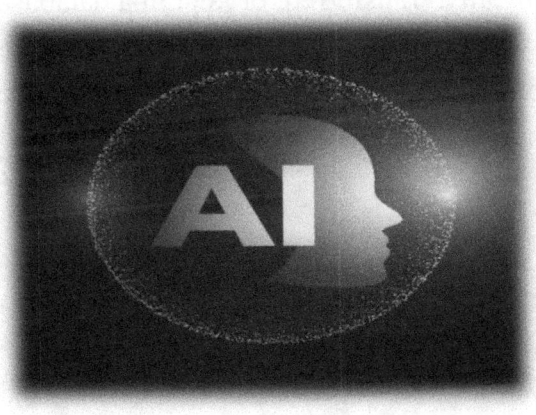

Annabel Hooper

## Copyright © 2024 by Annabel Hooper

All rights reserved. Replicating any portion of this book using mechanical, electronic, or other means is prohibited including information storage and retrieval systems, without the publisher's written consent, except for reviewers who may quote brief sections for their reviews. Therefore, the contents cannot be stored electronically, transferred, or kept in a database. The document cannot be copied either in part or in full, scanned, faxed, or retained without approval from the publisher or creator.

## Disclaimer

This book is designed solely for informational purposes. While every attempt has been made to assure the authenticity of the information, the author and publisher accept no responsibility for any losses or damages coming from the use of this content. It is recommended that before making any financial or business choices, readers carry out independent research and speak with a financial counselor or other professional.

# Table of Contents

**INTRODUCTION** ............................................................. 5

**14 WAYS TO MAKE MONEY WITH AI** ........................ 7

   1. Offer Writing Services with AI Writing Tools ............... 7
   2. Develop Apps with AI Coding Tools ............................. 9
   3. Manage Paid Advertising with AI ................................ 11
   4. Earn as a CRM & Sales Consultant ............................. 12
   5. Freelance as a Photo Editor ....................................... 14
   6. Consult as a Data Scientist ......................................... 15
   7. Provide AI Chatbots for Businesses ............................ 16
   8. Manage Social Media Brands ..................................... 17
   9. As a Freelancer, Edit Audio and Music ....................... 18
   10. Offer AI Translation Services .................................... 20
   11. Offer Multiple SEO Services ..................................... 21
   12. Become an AI-Powered Affiliate Marketer ................ 22
   13. Create and Sell AI-Generated Artwork ..................... 23
   14. Start a Web Design Business .................................... 25

**THE REALITY OF LEVERAGING AI FOR INCOME** ........... 26

**CHOOSING YOUR PATH TO PROFITABLE AI INTEGRATION** ................................................................. 29

   Key Takeaways .............................................................. 29
   Practical Steps ............................................................... 30

**FREQUENTLY ASKED QUESTIONS (FAQS)** ................... 32

**ABOUT THE AUTHOR** .................................................. 35

# INTRODUCTION

At one point, I found myself completely broke and unclear of how to turn things around. Then I realized the possibilities of AI. With a mix of interest and drive, I started researching AI technologies and applications. I established many web businesses, ranging from AI-generated artwork to automated SEO services.

My efforts paid off gradually, and I progressed from struggling financially to outstanding success. My transformational experience using the power of AI demonstrates the possibilities it has for everyone ready to accept it. This book outlines the 14 greatest strategies and tools for making money online with AI, providing a framework for others to follow.

Artificial Intelligence (AI) is becoming a game-changer in the business world. It supports entrepreneurs with tasks ranging from data analysis to content creation and marketing strategy development. AI is a fantastic way to save money, but being a relatively new technology, it can be a bit daunting to implement.

This book will guide you through fourteen ways to use AI to boost your income, whether you're a beginner or an expert. When used correctly, AI can help businesses and freelancers generate thousands of dollars each month at a surprisingly low cost. We've combined our expertise to present some of the best money-making opportunities with AI, using top-notch AI-powered tools.

These aren't your run-of-the-mill ChatGPT tricks; we've curated real business and side gig options you can start right now. Remember, no magic AI tool instantly deposits money into your account. However, AI can significantly enhance your productivity.

To effectively make money with AI, focus on applications that save time, improve your skills, cut costs, and create new opportunities. Let's dive into these AI money-making strategies - you'll be well on your way to earning your first dollar with AI!

# 14 WAYS TO MAKE MONEY WITH AI

Here are fourteen ideas to help you earn money using AI. All of these are available to anybody trying to earn legitimate money online, but they do require access to an AI tool and some strategic preparation. Even if you don't turn these ideas into a business or side hustle, they can still enhance your productivity.

## 1. Offer Writing Services with AI Writing Tools

- **Content Creation:**
Content creation is crucial in digital marketing, requiring substantial time and creative energy. The process involves brainstorming, researching, drafting, editing, publishing, and analyzing results, which can span from hours to months. AI has been instrumental in streamlining this process, especially with tools like ChatGPT and Jasper AI, which are popular for creating various types of content.

- **Freelance Writing with AI:**
Freelance writing, one of the oldest online money-making methods, has a low barrier to entry and minimal startup costs. AI can enhance your writing efficiency and research quality, making it a valuable tool for freelance writers.

Businesses need high-quality content for blogs, social media, and reports to improve search engine rankings, engage audiences, and establish industry authority. As a freelance writer, you can use AI tools to assist in creating engaging, fresh content that meets these needs.

However, relying entirely on AI for content creation can backfire. The key is to use AI intelligently throughout the writing process to enhance your output and meet client expectations.

By mastering AI writing tools, you can open up lucrative opportunities in content creation, helping businesses stand out in crowded niches and climb search engine ranks. This approach boosts your productivity and allows you to offer valuable services to clients, ultimately increasing your earning potential.

- **Copywriting with AI:**
Copywriting is a high-pressure but lucrative writing niche. It involves crafting compelling content that drives action, such as newsletters, sales pages, and cold emails. With AI, even those new to the field can learn and enhance their

copywriting skills. The rising demand for personalized, engaging content means freelancers who master AI tools can deliver results that boost clients' revenue.

AI can help with several elements of copywriting:

- Newsletters and Sales Pages: AI tools can help generate engaging copy for newsletters and landing pages, driving higher engagement and conversion rates.
- Cold Emails: AI can assist in crafting personalized cold emails, increasing the likelihood of positive responses and opening doors to new business opportunities.

To succeed in AI-assisted copywriting, continually improve your skills, use AI tools wisely, and maintain good client relationships. Recommended tools include Jasper, HoppyCopy, and Writesonic. Platforms like Resume.io can help you specialize in resume and cover letter writing, offering another lucrative niche.

## 2. Develop Apps with AI Coding Tools

Developing a Software as a Service (SaaS) product traditionally involves ideation, design, coding, testing, and launching, often taking months or years. AI can significantly streamline this process, helping you develop and launch products faster.

- **AI Coding Assistants:**
AI coding tools like GitHub Copilot can accelerate development by providing real-time code suggestions, automating repetitive tasks, and assisting with debugging. This enables you to create a minimum viable product (MVP) quickly and start selling it to early adopters. A great example is Louis Pereira's AudioPen, an AI-powered audio notemaker app that achieved rapid success.

- **No-Code App Building Tools:**
Platforms like Bubble and Directual allow for low-code app development. ChatGPT can assist with technical questions, helping you learn as you build. By focusing on creating an app that excels at one function, you can attract a loyal subscriber base and generate monthly recurring revenue (MRR).

The demand for niche SaaS products is growing, making product development a lucrative opportunity. Whether you're an experienced developer or a novice, leveraging AI can boost your productivity and help you bring products to market more quickly.

- **Freelance Coding:**
Freelancing can be a great alternative if you're skilled in coding but lack the time or passion to create your own AI app or startup. Freelance coding allows you to specialize in specific tasks and tech stacks that interest you.

A powerful strategy to maximize your profits as a freelancer is to productize your skills.

As a coding freelancer, you can choose to develop front-end web applications with React for small businesses needing customer review collection on their websites. By niching down, you can quickly become efficient in creating solutions for a specific need. After completing a few projects, you'll be able to package your solutions as plugins or extensions, making implementation easier for your clients and increasing your earning potential.

## 3. Manage Paid Advertising with AI

Digital marketing is complex, requiring a deep understanding of platforms, channels, and strategies. AI marketing tools can automate many tasks, create campaigns, analyze results, and optimize strategies based on predictive analytics.

- **Social Media Advertising with AI:**

Advertising on platforms like Facebook, Instagram, and Twitter involves creating and managing campaigns to reach targeted audiences. AI tools like Adzooma automate and optimize ad delivery by analyzing engagement data.

Tools like Lately and Pencil help create compelling ad content using data from previous campaigns. AI enhances ad placement and effectiveness, but human insight is still crucial for final creative input and strategy adjustments.

- **Search Advertising with AI:**
Search advertising targets users based on their search queries within search engine results. AI tools like WordStream, Acquisio, and Optmyzr streamline keyword selection, optimize bids, and predict ad performance, making campaigns more cost-effective.

AI tailors ads to individual users based on search behaviors, enhancing relevance. Continuous monitoring and adjustments are necessary to keep up with market trends and search engine algorithm changes. Digital marketers can leverage AI to deliver better client results more efficiently.

## 4. Earn as a CRM & Sales Consultant

Sales operations involve repetitive tasks like managing leads, tracking sales, analyzing performance data, and maintaining clean lists. These tasks can detract from the time salespeople could spend building relationships and closing deals. This presents an opportunity to create a service-based business or consulting service at the intersection of AI and Customer Relationship Management (CRM).

- **AI and CRM:**
AI can automate and streamline many CRM tasks, freeing up time for more strategic activities. As a CRM & Sales Consultant, you can help businesses implement AI tools to manage leads, track sales performance, and analyze data more effectively. Specializing in a particular area of CRM, such as lead management or sales analytics, can make your services more valuable. Complex software or processes often present opportunities to earn handsomely by offering specialized expertise.

- **Configure and Automate CRM Workflows:**
Customer Relationship Management (CRM) tools are crucial for businesses to stay organized and effectively engage with customers. However, many businesses struggle with poorly planned CRMs and messy data. AI sales tools like Apollo, Seamless AI, and Sendspark can enrich sales and contact management tasks by finding leads, tracking sales, analyzing performance data, and providing insights to improve sales strategies.

The challenge is that many businesses are unaware of these tools or face a steep learning curve in implementing them. By mastering a few CRM tools and their AI integrations, you can offer high-ticket services to businesses that need technical expertise. Specializing in a single CRM and a specific AI integration can make your services more valuable.

This is a lucrative opportunity because businesses are always looking to increase sales efficiency and need reliable partners to help them navigate the technology and strategy. You may also work as an integration expert with technologies like ActivePieces or Make, which connect different SaaS platforms and combine AI services like OpenAI and Anthropic. This allows you to help companies infuse their workflows with AI insights and decision-making.

## 5. Freelance as a Photo Editor

Professional photo editing is a meticulous process that enhances colors, adjusts lighting, removes unwanted elements, and more. AI photo enhancers like Topaz Photo AI, Photoshop Generative Fill, and Luminar can speed up this process, allowing you to edit more photos in less time without compromising quality. These tools can automate enhancements and even upscale images, making bulk editing possible.

- **Work with Photographers:**

Photographers often seek professional image editors to handle high volumes of photos from shoots. This allows them to focus on client interactions and photoshoots. AI tools can assist in adapting to different styles required by photographers' clients. Adobe Lightroom, with its AI image editing tools, is an excellent starting point for mastering photo editing with AI.

- **Edit Product Photos for E-commerce:**
  With the rise of eCommerce, there is a growing demand for professional product images. Great product photos are essential for capturing attention and driving sales. AI tools can help remove and replace backgrounds, enhance overall image quality, and make product photos more appealing. Whether you are a photographer or a graphic designer, leveraging AI photo enhancers can increase your productivity and client base. It's not too late to start mastering these tools and capitalizing on the growing eCommerce market.

## 6. Consult as a Data Scientist

With the advent of machine learning, tools like ChatGPT have become invaluable for data science and research, particularly in pattern recognition. ChatGPT's official data and code plugin, Data Analyst, significantly streamlines data processing and analysis workflows. This tool can:

- ❖ Convert file formats (TSV, YAML, CSV, JSON)
- ❖ Generate summary graphs and charts to visualize data trends
- ❖ Perform various statistical analyses
- ❖ Create SQL tables and schemas from file contents

- ❖ Identify suitable data types for each column
- ❖ Conduct thorough error checks to pinpoint missing data or irregular characters

Using ChatGPT's Python environment, data scientists can automate repetitive tasks and create repeatable solutions, saving considerable time and effort. This makes consulting as a data scientist an exciting and lucrative opportunity, even if it's not the most glamorous job.

Data analytics offers many niches to specialize in, such as GIS/location data, technical SEO and ranking data, business intelligence (BI), medical/scientific data, and eCommerce product database data. By focusing on a niche, you can refine automated processes and scripts to enhance your efficiency and value to clients.

## 7. Provide AI Chatbots for Businesses

Customer service is crucial for businesses but can be overwhelming due to the volume of inquiries. AI chatbots offer a solution by handling simple inbound inquiries 24/7, providing instant relief for businesses. AI chatbots can:

- ❖ Answer common questions
- ❖ Guide users through troubleshooting processes
- ❖ Assist with sales and bookings

This allows businesses to focus on more complex customer service issues. Consulting and installing AI customer support software is a profitable opportunity because many businesses need this technology but lack the expertise to implement it. By specializing in AI chatbot configuration, you can offer valuable services to clients.

To get started, explore platforms like Chatbase, Tidio, Botsonic, and Botsify (which offers white-labeling options ideal for agencies or freelancers). Gather a knowledge base and internal documents to train the chatbot, then integrate it with your client's website to meet their satisfaction.

Specializing in a few platforms and becoming proficient in conversational AI technology can make you an indispensable partner for businesses looking to enhance their customer service operations.

## 8. Manage Social Media Brands

For many business owners, managing social media is a tedious task that distracts from running their core business. Understanding various platforms, creating engaging content, and managing online communities requires significant time and effort. AI social media management tools can simplify this process by automating post creation and scheduling, managing inbox conversations, and providing analytics on post-performance.

- **AI Tools for Social Media Management:**
If you are interested in managing social media accounts for small businesses and brands, AI tools can make the job more manageable. Tools like Ocoya can help streamline social media management, making it easier to handle multiple brands and help them achieve their business objectives.

AI can assist in every aspect of social media management, from content creation to engagement and analytics, increasing productivity and attracting more clients.

- **Social Media Video Creation and Editing:**
Creating engaging social media videos is a key strategy for businesses and influencers, but video editing can be challenging and time-consuming. AI video editing tools can simplify the video creation process, allowing you to produce high-quality videos quickly.

Tools like FlexClip can help you edit videos by trimming footage, adding effects and transitions, and syncing audio, making video editing accessible even to those with minimal experience. These tools can also break down longer videos into shorter clips suitable for platforms like YouTube Shorts and Instagram Reels.

## 9. As a Freelancer, Edit Audio and Music

The creator economy is booming, offering numerous opportunities for those interested in audio-based services.

Whether you're helping YouTubers, podcasters, musicians, or other creatives, AI technologies can enhance your workflow and expand your service offerings.

- **Generate Music and Background Tracks:**
AI music generators like AIVA and Mubert can create unique music tracks in various styles and moods, suitable for videos, games, or other media projects. These tools allow you to generate music quickly and experiment with different musical ideas, streamlining the composition process. By leveraging AI, you can offer music and background track creation services on freelance marketplaces like Fiverr, reaching a broad audience and growing your business.

- **Audio Editing Services for Podcasters:**
AI tools play a significant role in refining and enhancing audio content for podcasts, ensuring a professional listening experience. Tools like Descript offer features such as automatic transcriptions, voice cloning, and easy audio editing as if it were text. Resound provides AI-driven audio enhancement, optimizing sound quality by adjusting levels, removing background noise, and improving clarity. Exemplary AI automates routine editing tasks, allowing you to focus on the creative aspects of podcast production.

By using AI tools for audio editing, you can help podcasters produce high-quality content efficiently. Transcriptions enhance accessibility and SEO for podcast and YouTube content, while voice cloning enables creators to generate content in their voice without extensive recording setups. AI audio editing tools enable you to assist more clients with important tasks, contributing to their projects or businesses effectively.

## 10. Offer AI Translation Services

As businesses expand globally, the demand for translation services has skyrocketed. Human translation can be time-consuming and expensive, especially for large volumes of text. AI translation tools significantly speed up this process, providing a good starting point for human translators. While AI translations might not always be perfect, they can handle the bulk of the work, allowing human translators to fine-tune the results for accuracy and nuance.

- **Combining AI and Human Translation:**

If you are multilingual, you can offer a competitive mix of AI and human translation services. Use AI tools like Copy.ai to translate large text blocks quickly, then use your language skills to refine the output. This hybrid approach ensures high-quality translations at a lower cost. Additionally, familiarize yourself with popular translation plugins for platforms like WordPress, as these are commonly used by businesses for multilingual website content.

# 11. Offer Multiple SEO Services

Search Engine Optimization (SEO) is a complex and essential task for businesses aiming to improve their online visibility. SEO involves optimizing websites to rank higher on search engines, requiring a deep understanding of algorithms, content strategies, and technical optimization.

- **Using AI for SEO:**

AI tools like Semrush, SurferSEO, and AlliSEO can streamline many SEO tasks, including keyword research, content optimization, and performance tracking. These tools can also assist with more complex aspects of SEO, such as link building and technical audits. While AI tools are not a replacement for human expertise, they significantly simplify the traditional role of an SEO specialist, making it easier to handle multiple clients and tasks efficiently.

- **The Demand for SEO Services:**

SEO is in high demand, and there are surprisingly few qualified practitioners. By leveraging AI tools, you can offer effective SEO services to businesses, helping them improve their online presence and drive more traffic to their websites. If you run your own website, using these tools can also enhance your SEO efforts, generating more traffic and potential revenue.

## 12. Become an AI-Powered Affiliate Marketer

Affiliate marketing involves promoting other people's products and earning a commission on sales. While the field is competitive, AI can provide a significant edge in identifying lucrative products, creating content, and automating marketing efforts.

- **Leveraging AI in Affiliate Marketing:**

AI tools can help you find high-converting products, create engaging content, and manage email marketing campaigns. With an affiliate website and an AI writer, you can produce high-quality reviews, comparisons, and how-to articles that attract and convert readers. Platforms like WordPress offer numerous affiliate plugins to support your technical needs.

- **Building a Successful Affiliate Marketing Site:**

To succeed in affiliate marketing, focus on creating valuable content that helps your audience make informed purchasing decisions. Building an audience and establishing a strong SEO profile takes time, so approach this as a long-term side hustle. Start with a niche you are passionate about, such as AI chatbots, which are currently in high demand. With consistent effort and high-quality content, your affiliate website can become a lucrative income source.

## 13. Create and Sell AI-Generated Artwork

The explosion of AI art has revolutionized the art industry, offering new opportunities and marketplaces for creative expression. Traditionally, artists spend a significant amount of time developing concepts, creating artwork, and finding ways to sell their pieces. With AI design tools, anyone can generate unique art quickly and efficiently. Tools like ChatGPT's DALL-E 3 or alternatives such as MidJourney and Stable Diffusion allow users to create stunning visuals in minutes. However, producing marketable AI art requires skillful prompt engineering and a keen understanding of artistic trends.

- **AI-Generated Stickers:**

AI can produce incredible images suitable for physical stickers. Using an AI image generator, you can create characters, animals, or any other design. For best results, use a background removal tool like Adobe's background remover to isolate the image. Afterward, use a sticker printing service such as Custom Stickers to print your designs. Selling these stickers can be done through online platforms or local markets.

- **Use AI to Make Wall Art, Tapestries, and Posters:**

AI-generated art can also be used for posters, wall tapestries, coasters, and other mediums. These formats can handle complex and colorful designs, making them perfect for AI art. While T-shirts have printing limitations, posters and tapestries are more accommodating. Once you create your art, pair it with a print-on-demand service like Printify to sell on your online store or an eCommerce platform like Etsy.

**Pro-Tip:**

- Pair with Print-On-Demand Services: Using services like Printify can streamline the process of selling AI art. They handle printing and shipping, allowing you to focus on creating and marketing your designs.
- Avoid Intellectual Property Infringement: Create original ideas rather than replicating popular characters like Mickey Mouse. This not only avoids legal issues but also encourages unique and marketable creations.
- Competitive Market: AI-generated art is a highly competitive niche. Success requires a good go-to-market plan and a distinctive artistic style.

By honing your skills in AI art and finding the right niche, you can turn this modern technology into a profitable venture. Whether through stickers, posters, or other mediums, AI art offers endless possibilities for creative entrepreneurs.

# 14. Start a Web Design Business

Nowadays, it's imperative for businesses to have a strong internet presence. A well-designed website draws users in, holds their interest, and eventually wins them over as clients. As a web design professional, you can meet this demand by creating and maintaining websites. WordPress, with its flexibility, is an excellent platform for building any website. Adding a theme builder like Divi enhances its capabilities, making design easier and more flexible.

- **Utilize AI in Web Design:**

    - Divi AI: This tool integrates advanced AI image editing, content writing, and layout/page creation into WordPress. It simplifies the design process and allows for the creation of stunning websites with less effort.

    - AI Plugins and Builders: Tools like WPTurbo and CodeWP help you create custom plugins for WordPress, further enhancing your website's functionality. AI-driven design tools can generate high-quality designs and write compelling landing page copy, streamlining the website creation process.

Starting a web design business with these tools can help you offer more value to your clients and handle more projects efficiently.

# THE REALITY OF LEVERAGING AI FOR INCOME

AI is a powerful technology that can enhance efficiency and productivity. However, it is not a magic wand or a Get-Rich-Quick solution. Success with AI requires pairing it with legitimate business ideas and hard work. AI is best used to enhance skills, offer better services, and create more value.

**Tips for Using AI to Make Money:**

1. Look for Specialized Tasks: AI excels when focused on specific processes or outcomes. Break down your use of AI into its smallest parts to maximize its effectiveness.

2. Tools ≠ Tasks: Owning an AI tool doesn't automatically generate income. Tools need to be used skillfully to achieve desired results.

3. Money is Found in the Hard Tasks: While AI can simplify many tasks, the real money lies in hard work or tasks that require experience. Success requires effort and expertise.

4. When You Provide Value, You are Rewarded: Use AI to create real value, whether through products or services. When you provide valuable solutions, people are willing to pay for them.

5. Constant Learning and Adaptation: AI is an ever-changing field. To keep competitive, be informed on the most recent developments, instruments, and best practices. Spending time learning new abilities and adjusting to changes will enable you to more wisely apply artificial intelligence.

6. Identify Market Gaps: Use artificial intelligence to examine market trends and find underserved or unmet demands. This realization will enable you to develop original goods or services addressing certain pain issues, therefore acquiring a competitive advantage.

7. Automate Routine Tasks: Use artificial intelligence to automatically handle time-consuming and repetitive tasks. This not only increases productivity but also releases your time to concentrate on more strategic and creative projects meant to generate income.

8. Enhance Customer Experience: AI allows one to customize client contacts and raise the quality of services utilizing its use. AI-driven customer assistance, recommendation systems, and chatbots all help to raise customer satisfaction and loyalty, hence boosting sales and repeat business.

9. Leverage Data insights: Utilizing AI-powered analytics to get thorough understanding of consumer behavior, industry trends, and corporate performance. More efficient tactics, better-targeted marketing, and improved operations may all follow from data-driven decisions.

10. Network and Collaborate: Work with other companies, artificial intelligence consultants, and tech communities to provide information and resources. While networking may offer great chances and insights, collaboration can result in creative ideas and create new revenue sources.

# CHOOSING YOUR PATH TO PROFITABLE AI INTEGRATION

AI is transforming various fields, from writing to art, coding to marketing. Understanding how to leverage AI for financial gain can provide a significant advantage in your career and personal endeavors. The goal of using AI isn't to replace humans or to create passive income streams without effort. Instead, AI should augment human capabilities, helping us achieve more and reach new heights. We hope the ideas presented have been valuable and inspire you to take meaningful steps toward incorporating AI into your income-generating strategies.

## Key Takeaways

1. Diverse Opportunities: AI provides a wide range of revenue streams, from building AI tools and handling sponsored adverts to freelancing as a picture editor or offering AI translation services. By mastering specialized skills and niches, you may carve out a lucrative route.

2. Increased Productivity: AI technologies such as ChatGPT, Descript, and numerous AI art producers may dramatically improve your productivity. These tools help you simplify complicated operations and produce high-quality outcomes more effectively.

3. The Importance of Human knowledge: While AI can do a variety of activities, human knowledge remains critical. Combining AI with your existing talents and expertise can result in better outcomes and more client satisfaction.

4. Passive Income Potential: AI may produce passive revenue through activities like affiliate marketing, digital product sales, and the creation and sale of AI-generated artwork. The objective is to develop valuable content that will generate income over time.

5. Continuous learning: The AI landscape is continuously changing. Keeping up with the newest technologies, trends, and approaches can allow you to remain ahead of the competition and continuously improve your products.

## Practical Steps

1. Choose a Niche: Determine where you want to use AI, whether it's writing, art, computing, marketing, or another sector. Specializing in a certain area can enable you to

establish yourself as an expert and attract additional customers.

2. Master AI Tools: Invest time in studying and mastering the AI tools that are relevant to your field. The better you grasp these tools, the more efficiently you can utilize them to produce high-quality outcomes.

3. Create a Portfolio: A professional portfolio is a great way to showcase your work and expertise. This will assist you attract customers and illustrate the value you can offer.

4. Market Your Services: Use internet platforms, social media, and networking to promote your services. Highlight how AI improves your job and what clients might expect.

5. Provide Value: Concentrate on giving genuine value to your clients. Whether you're refining their sales procedures, increasing their web presence, or generating spectacular images, your objective should be to have a beneficial influence on their business.

# FREQUENTLY ASKED QUESTIONS (FAQs)

**1. Is it possible to make money with AI?**

Certainly! Making money with AI is an exciting possibility. There are several ways you can capitalize on this rapidly growing technology. Each of them requires narrowing down to specific tasks that are ideal for AI to perform. Our favorites are developing with AI, writing with AI, and managing paid ads.

**2. How can I make passive income with AI?**

If you are looking to generate passive income using AI, there are plenty of opportunities out there. Here are a few ways to consider:

- ❖ Create and Sell Digital Products or Courses: Use AI tools to develop educational content or digital products that can be sold repeatedly.
- ❖ AI-Generated Art: Create and sell digital art using AI art generator tools. AI marketplaces for buying and selling AI art can help generate passive income.
- ❖ Affiliate Marketing: With AI tools for website creation, writing, and SEO, it is possible to start an affiliate marketing website that generates passive revenue.

Just remember, the key to passive income is to take the time to create something that holds value over the long haul.

### 3. Can I make money with AI bots?

There are multiple ways to make money using AI chatbots:

- Build Chatbots for Businesses: You can sell installation services for chatbots that provide customer service, set appointments, qualify leads, and answer questions. Depending on the complexity, you can charge between $100 to $400 or more.
- Sell AI Bot Templates: Create a collection of templates for different types of bots and sell them multiple times to generate passive income. These templates usually include a base prompt that guides the chatbot to answer in specific ways.

### 4. How can I make money on YouTube with AI?

AI revolutionizes YouTube content creation and optimization by:

- Drafting scripts and descriptions.
- Automating video editing tasks like adding music and subtitles.
- Providing insights into viewership patterns to optimize posting schedules.

Using AI for these tasks saves time, enhances productivity, and allows for more frequent video uploads. This also opens opportunities for outsourcing, appealing to businesses seeking efficient content strategies.

**5. How do I make money online as told by Redditors?**

Reddit is a great place to discover the best ideas for making money. Based on numerous subreddits, many people are finding success with AI through:

- Data analysis.
- SEO services.
- Developing and selling their software.

However, be cautious of false claims promising quick riches with AI. The most successful strategies involve providing real value and leveraging AI to enhance existing skills and services.

# About the Author

Annabel Hooper is a passionate entrepreneur and technology enthusiast keen to leverage artificial intelligence to achieve financial success. She has years of experience in digital marketing, web design, and data science, and has helped countless individuals and businesses achieve their goals by leveraging the power of AI. Annabel's practical views and hands-on approach make her a well-known authority in the sector. "Flat Broke to Billionaire" is her latest project to help others transform their financial destinies.

# Appreciation

*Thank you for taking the time to read* **"Flat Broke to Billionaire."** *Your opinions are really valuable to me. If this book was helpful to you, please think about giving it an Amazon review. The information you provide enables me to do better and helps other readers find fresh approaches to achieving financial success.*

www.ingramcontent.com/pod-product-compliance
Lightning Source LLC
Chambersburg PA
CBHW072056230526
45479CB00010B/1109